SEALS AND SEA LIONS

SEALS AND SEA LIONS

CHARLES ROTTER
PHOTOS BY MARTY SNYDERMAN

THE CHILD'S WORLD

DESIGN
Bill Foster of Albarella & Associates, Inc.

This book is a presentation of Newfield Publications, Inc.
For information about Newfield Publications book clubs for children
write to: **Newfield Publications, Inc.,**
4343 Equity Drive, Columbus, Ohio 43228.

Published by arrangement with The Child's World, Inc.
Newfield Publications is a federally registered
trademark of Newfield Publications, Inc.

1996 edition

Library of Congress Cataloging-in-Publication Data
Rotter, Charles.
Seals and Sea Lions/Charles Rotter.
p. cm. — (Child's World Wildlife Library)
Summary: Examines the physical characteristics, habitats, and behavior of
seals and sea lions and discusses the differences between them..
ISBN 0-89565-714-7
1. Seals (Animals) — Juvenile literature. 2. Sea Lions — Juvenile literature.
[1. Seals. (Animals)   2. Sea Lions.]
I. Title.
II. Series.   91-3076
QL737.P6R65 1991   CIP
599.74'5—dc20   AC

For Mom and Dad

What was that? Was it a flash of light on the water? The first time you see a seal or a sea lion you might make that mistake. Seals and sea lions are so quick and smooth, they glide easily through the water. Even when moving very fast, they can stop, turn, and speed away in the blink of an eye.

Seals and sea lions usually live along coastlines, especially in colder seas. One reason they can live in cold seas is that they are covered with thick fur. Their fur helps to keep in body heat, protecting the animals from the cold water. Seals and sea lions stay warm another way, too. They have a layer of fat under their skin called *blubber*. Blubber keeps in body heat so that seals and sea lions stay warm in the cold water.

Can you tell which
of these animals are
seals and which are
sea lions?

How can you tell the difference between seals and sea lions? Just look at their ears. True seals are called *earless seals* because they don't have ears sticking out from their heads. Sea lions are called *eared seals* because they have ears you can see.

Another difference between seals and sea lions is the way they swim. Seals swim almost the same way as fish or dolphins. They push themselves through the water with their tails. Sea lions, however, flap their front flippers the way birds flap their wings. They use their front flippers to pull themselves through the water.

There are many different types of both seals and sea lions. Some seals can dive very deep and stay underwater for a whole hour! Other types can be very big. Here we see an elephant seal. It is the biggest type of seal. See how much larger it is than the scientist. This type of seal can weigh four tons. That's as much as a truck!

In the warmer waters off the coast of California, there is a lush underwater forest. This forest doesn't have trees like a forest on land. Instead, it is made of kelp. Kelp lives in the ocean and grows tall, just like trees. It grows from the sea bottom toward the water's surface. Many types of animals live in the kelp forest, so it is a good hunting ground for California sea lions.

Seals and sea lions are *carnivorous*. That means they eat other animals. This sea lion is chasing its next meal. Because they hunt in the sea, seals and sea lions eat lots of fish. They also eat other sea creatures, such as shrimp, crabs, and even octopuses. Seals can feel with their whiskers the way we feel with our fingers. Seals use their whiskers to find food and to avoid underwater traffic accidents.

Seals and sea lions can be very playful. They chase and dodge each other. They like to play with people, too. This California sea lion is teasing the scuba diver.

Though seals and sea lions spend much of their lives in the water, they're not fish. They breathe air just as we do. This scuba diver gets air from the tank, but seals have to come to the surface to breathe. When seals and sea lions need to rest, they come out of the water onto land.

Seals and sea lions often group together. They rest on the rocks and lounge in the sun. Male seals are called *bulls*. Bulls will claim an area of land as their own. The bulls let females into their area. They patrol the area to keep out any other males. If challenged by another bull, they will fight to defend their piece of land.

Seals have their babies on land. Most mother seals have only one baby. Seal and sea lion babies are called *pups*. A mother seal will take care of its pup for several weeks, until the pup can take care of itself. This mother seal is feeding her pup milk, just as many land animals do. She not only feeds it, she protects it from enemies, too.

A seal pup can swim as soon as it is born. But newborn baby seals are not very strong swimmers. Before they can take care of themselves, baby seals have to grow strong and fat enough to float easily in the water. This young pup is taking a nap. The seal pup grows strong and fat quickly. In several weeks, it will be swimming, playing, and hunting for its own meals.

Seals and sea lions have enemies. Just as some animals are food for seals, seals are food for other animals. On northern coastlines, seals have to watch out for polar bears. Sharks and killer whales also will attack and eat seals and sea lions. Sea lions are quick swimmers, though. It's not easy for the slow-moving sharks to catch them.

Seals' and sea lions' biggest enemy is not another wild animal. The worst danger to seals and sea lions comes from people. For many years, people have killed seals to eat and to make clothes from their fur. Some types of seals are in danger of being wiped out completely.

There are now many laws to protect seals and sea lions from people. Hunting is still allowed, but only in certain places and at certain times. But our world is very big. Laws passed in one part of the world cannot always protect animals in another part of the world.

Seals and sea lions are beautiful and often friendly animals. Like all wild creatures, they are an important part of life on earth. If enough people care, they can be protected. Then we can enjoy seeing them swim and play for years to come.